10-05

DISCARD

**Explorers!**

# Hernán Cortés
## Conquistador and Explorer

*Arlene Bourgeois Molzahn*

**Enslow Publishers, Inc.**

40 Industrial Road      PO Box 38
Box 398      Aldershot
Berkeley Heights, NJ 07922      Hants GU12 6BP
USA      UK

http://www.enslow.com

*To my son Kenny who shares my love for history.*

**Library of Congress Cataloging-in-Publication Data**

Molzahn, Arlene Bourgeois.
    Hernán Cortés : conquistador and explorer / Arlene Bourgeois Molzahn.
       p. cm. — (Explorers!)
    Includes bibliographical references and index.
    ISBN 0-7660-2069-X
    1. Cortés, Hernán, 1485–1547—Juvenile literature. 2. Mexico—History—Conquest, 1519–1540—Juvenile literature. 3. Mexico—Discovery and exploration—Spanish—Juvenile literature. 4. Hispaniola—Discovery and exploration—Spanish—Juvenile literature. 5. Conquerors—Mexico—Juvenile literature. 6. Explorers—America—Juvenile literature. 7. Explorers—Spain—Juvenile literature. I. Enslow Publishers. II. Title. III. Explorers! (Enslow Publishers)
F1230.C385 M65 2003
972'.02'092—dc21                                           2002005316

Printed in the United States of America

10 9 8 7 6 5 4 3 2 1

**To Our Readers:** We have done our best to make sure all Internet Addresses in this book were active and appropriate when we went to press. However, the author and the publisher have no control over and assume no liability for the material available on those Internet sites or on other Web sites they may link to. Any comments or suggestions can be sent by e-mail to comments@enslow.com or to the address on the back cover.

Every effort has been made to locate all copyright holders of material used in this book. If any errors or omissions have occurred, corrections will be made in future editions of this book.

**Illustration Credits:** © 1999 Artville, LLC., pp. 4, 21; Corel Corporation, pp. 18, 19 (bottom), 42, 43; Enslow Publishers, Inc., p. 22 (top), 39 (top); Library of Congress, pp. 1, 6, 7, 8, 9, 10, 12, 13, 14, 15, 16, 19 (top), 20, 22 (bottom), 24, 25, 26, 27, 28, 30, 31, 32, 33, 35, 36, 38, 39 (bottom), 40, 41.

**Cover Illustration:** background, Monster Zero Media; portrait from the Library of Congress.

Please note: Compasses on the cover and in the book are from © 1999 Artville, LLC.

# Contents

Mexico is a part of
North America.

# The Beautiful City

In 1325, the Aztec people lived on the land we today call Mexico. They wandered from place to place. The Aztecs finally settled in the Valley of Mexico where they built a city.

They called it Tenochtitlán (tay nohch TEE tlahn). It became their capital city. Tenochtitlán was built on an island in a small lake. Roadways connected the island to the mainland. The main streets of the city were straight and wide. There were huge pyramids, castles, and gardens. There were busy marketplaces and many temples.

The Aztecs built floating gardens.

The Aztecs grew corn, beans, sweet potatoes, tomatoes, and cotton. They built a water system that brought fresh water from the mainland to the island city. This same water system brought water to their crops.

The food the Aztecs ate was spicy. They made a pancake called *tlaxcalli*, or tortilla. The Aztecs would wrap the tlaxcalli around vegetables and meat to make a taco.

Sometimes the Aztec people had a chocolate drink. Only rich people could afford to drink it all the time.

Many foods that we eat today are from the Aztecs. Chili, chocolate, and tacos are very popular. Some English words also come from the Aztecs, like avocado and tomato.

The Aztecs had a calendar based on 365 days in one year, which is similar to our calendar.

They had no money system. But they sometimes used cacao beans and other goods like we use money today. The Aztecs also traded goods for things they needed.

This illustration shows the Aztec creation of Tenochtitlán.

performed human sacrifices. This means that they killed people to please their gods. They believed that their gods needed human sacrifices to stay strong.

The Aztec people believed that one of the gods had been driven from their country. Before he left, he promised he would return and take all of the Aztec lands and cities for himself. He would be a white man who came from the east. He would arrive from across the sea in the Aztec year called One Reed. One Reed was the European year 1519. In 1519, a white man, Hernán Cortés, arrived in Tenochtitlán from the east after crossing the sea. Many Aztec people believed he was that god.

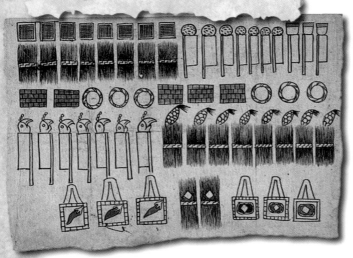

The Aztecs used pictures like these to help them keep track of goods.

# The Early Years

Hernán Cortés was born in 1485 in Medellín, Spain. His mother was Catalina and his father was Martin Cortés. Hernán was their only child. His father had been a captain in the Spanish army. But he and his wife did not want their son to become a soldier. Hernán always seemed to be sick as a child. His parents did not think that he would be in the army.

In 1499, when Hernán was fourteen years old, his parents sent him to a university in Salamanca. There he studied Latin, grammar, and law. He learned more about the Christian religion. His parents wanted him to become a lawyer. He studied at the university for two years. Cortés became bored with school and returned home without finishing.

Medellín was a small town filled with shepherds, farmers, and soldiers. The shepherds led a quiet life caring for their sheep. The farmers also led a quiet life harvesting wheat and grapes. Young Hernán did not want to be a shepherd or a farmer. And he did not want to be a lawyer. At sixteen-years-old, he felt that soldiers led a far more exciting life. He wanted a life of adventure.

These were exciting times for the people of Europe. Christopher Columbus had sailed west. He and his men told stories of the lands they

Many explorers of this time wanted to sail to new lands and teach people about the Christian religion.

Cortés became bored with school and returned home. He enjoyed watching ships come to port and listening to the sailors's stories about new lands.

Christopher Columbus discovered new lands as he was trying to find the Indies.

## Christopher Columbus (1451-1506)

Christopher Columbus was born in Genoa, Italy. Like many explorers of his time, he wanted to find an all-water route to the Indies. Columbus thought if he sailed west he would find the Indies. He actually landed on islands in the Caribbean Sea, which he thought were the Indies. Columbus went on four trips between 1492 and 1504. During these four trips, he explored what are today called the West Indies and the coasts of Central and South America.

had visited and of the people they had seen across the ocean. Cortés heard all these stories as he traveled throughout Spain. He watched ships come to port loaded with spices. He saw soldiers and sailors with their pockets filled with gold.

When he returned home, Cortés asked his parents for money for a trip across the great ocean. He hoped to see for himself the new lands Columbus had found. Cortés was a Christian and he wanted to bring his religion to the people of these lands.

Cortés might have seen ships like these coming to port loaded with spices and goods.

His mother and father could tell that Cortés would not be happy staying at home in Medellín. They gave him money for the trip. His mother also gave him a supply of jams and jellies to take along. In early 1504, Cortés boarded a Spanish ship and set sail.

In 1504, Hernán Cortés set sail looking for adventure.

Hernán Cortés was on a ship that was going to Hispaniola. This map is from about 1529.

# Hispaniola

In 1504, Cortés was on one of the five ships from Spain that was going to bring goods to Hispaniola. Hispaniola was a Spanish colony started by Christopher Columbus during one of his voyages. The Arawak people lived on the island. Today the island is the home of two countries, Haiti and the Dominican Republic.

Alonso Quintero, the captain of the ship Cortés was on, hoped to be the first to reach Hispaniola. Then he would get a better price for his goods. The five ships stopped at the Canary Islands to get food and fresh water before starting the voyage across the ocean. Quintero's

### Haiti

Haiti is a country in the West Indies. It is part of the island of Hispaniola. The other side of the island is the Dominican Republic. Haiti's capital is Port-au-Prince. Most people who live on Haiti are farmers. They raise beans, corn, rice, and yams. In the valleys and on the mountains of Haiti, people grow coffee, cacao (the bean used to make chocolate), and sugar cane.

ship set sail before the other four ships were ready to go.

Shortly after leaving port, the ship was struck by strong winds. The storm destroyed the sails. The captain slowly took his battered ship back to the Canary Islands. He begged the other captains to wait until his ship was repaired before leaving for Hispaniola. They agreed. The five ships left the Canary Islands together. They were out to sea only a few days when, in the middle of the night, a strong wind began to blow. Captain Quintero woke the ship's crew. He ordered his men to quickly raise the sails.

Then his ship quietly slipped away from the others.

Quintero and his crew became lost. Food was running out. Rainwater was collected and used for drinking. The men feared they would die at sea. Then one day a white dove was seen flying overhead. It sat on the mast and then flew off. Quintero ordered the ship to sail in the direction that the dove had gone. Four days later,

When Cortés arrived in Hispaniola he was given some land to farm.

## Dominican Republic

The Dominican Republic is a country in the West Indies. It is part of the island of Hispaniola. The other side of the island is Haiti. Santo Domingo is the capital of the Dominican Republic. There are many mountains in the Dominican Republic. Most people who live in rural areas are farmers. People who live in the cities earn a living by working in factories, for the government, or by fishing.

**Cortés took part in the capture of Cuba.**

the ship reached the island of Hispaniola. The other four ships had already reached shore and sold their goods.

As soon as Cortés arrived in Hispaniola, he went to the governor. Cortés was given a large amount of land.

He was also given people to work the land for him. But Cortés was not very happy. He did not want to be a farmer. He wanted to search for gold and become rich and powerful.

But Cortés decided to farm until something better came along. He raised hogs and made money selling salt pork to ships leaving the island.

The Spanish governor appointed Cortés to the town council. Cortés also went on several military expeditions to help keep the peace among the people of Hispaniola.

In 1511, Cortés took part in the Spanish capture of the island of Cuba. He was rewarded with more land and more workers. Cortés sent for cattle from Europe and started a herd. He also had people mine for gold on the land. Cortés lived in Cuba for seven years, and he became very rich.

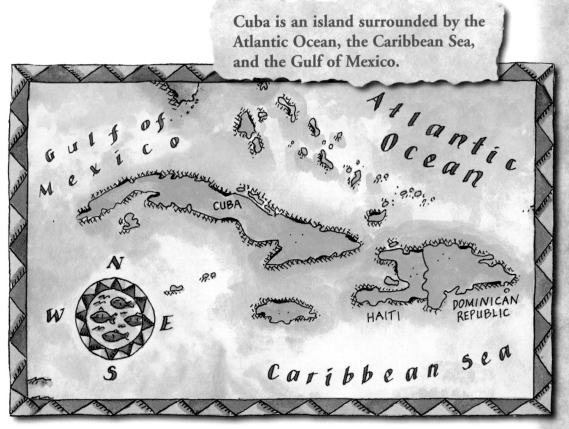

Cuba is an island surrounded by the Atlantic Ocean, the Caribbean Sea, and the Gulf of Mexico.

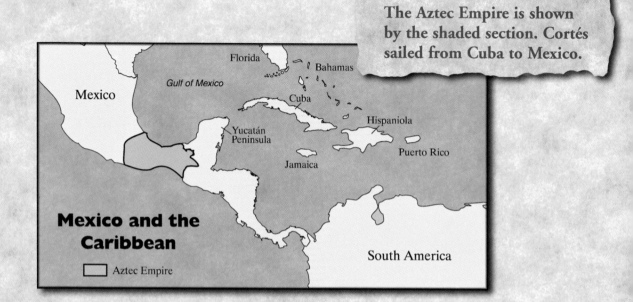

The Aztec Empire is shown by the shaded section. Cortés sailed from Cuba to Mexico.

Mexico and the Caribbean

☐ Aztec Empire

Florida
Gulf of Mexico
Bahamas
Mexico
Cuba
Yucatán Peninsula
Hispaniola
Puerto Rico
Jamaica
South America

While living in Cuba, Hernán Cortés heard about lands that had a lot of gold. He wanted to go to these lands.

# On to Mexico

While Cortés was living in Cuba, he heard of a land that was rich in gold and silver. That land today is now called Mexico. Cortés wanted to find the gold and silver. The governor of Cuba told Cortés he could lead an expedition to explore the land. Cortés also wanted to bring the Christian religion to the people.

Shortly before Cortés left, the governor changed his mind. He sent a message saying that Cortés was no longer in charge. But Cortés did not listen to the governor.

On February 18, 1519, Cortés set sail for Mexico with

a fleet of eleven ships. There were many sailors and soldiers. They brought weapons such as guns, cannons, and crossbows. Horses were brought along as well. The ships also carried wine, drinking water, beans, bread, and flour. They had pigs and chickens so the men could have meat to eat.

Cortés sailed along the coast of Mexico and stopped at a small town. Here they asked the people for food. Cortés also wanted to search the area for gold and silver.

**Cortés stopped at a small town in search of gold. The people wanted him to leave.**

The people did not want the Spaniards to enter their town. So the Spaniards attacked. The people fought hard. But, they had never seen horses. They believed that the man and the horse were one person. They also believed that this new strange person with six legs was a god and could not be killed. The Spaniards quickly overcame the people.

The explorers left the town. They kept sailing along the east coast of Mexico. One day, Aztecs in two canoes came to the ships. The Aztecs said they had come in the name of their chief, Montezuma. They brought gold and fancy feathered robes as gifts. The Spaniards fired one of the cannons. The Aztecs were very frightened. As soon as they left the ship, the Aztecs hurried to Tenochtitlán. They told Montezuma what they had seen.

Montezuma was the emperor of the Aztec people.

Montezuma feared that Hernán Cortés was the god who had promised to return to Tenochtitlán.

Montezuma feared that this was the god who had promised to return to Tenochtitlán. He sent one hundred people carrying more gifts of gold and silver to Cortés. They had a message for the Spaniards. The Spaniards would not be welcomed in Tenochtitlán. Montezuma wanted Cortés and his men to leave.

Cortés did not listen to Montezuma. He planned to take the city of Tenochtitlán. But he had two problems. He knew Montezuma had many great warriors who would protect the city. Also, many of the Spaniards wanted to return to Cuba. Before he started marching toward Tenochtitlán, Cortés had a few of his men set fire to the ships. Now his men would have to stay and fight because they had no way to return to Cuba.

Hernán Cortés ordered some of the ships burned so his men would stay and fight.

Hernán Cortés and his men
traveled about 250 miles to
reach Tenochtitlán.

Montezuma welcomed
Hernán Cortés and his men.

# The Capture of Tenochtitlán

Cortés and his men traveled about 250 miles to reach Tenochtitlán. The Spaniards went through many small towns along the way. Most of the people from these towns had been badly treated by Montezuma. Many joined Cortés and his men as they marched to the great city.

Early in the morning of November 8, 1519, Cortés and his army reached Tenochtitlán. People from the city came to meet them. They were dressed in fancy robes and colorful feathers. Among them was Montezuma. Cortés gave the emperor a necklace of glass beads.

Montezuma welcomed Cortés and gave him two beautiful gold necklaces. He also gave Cortés and his soldiers a beautiful palace to live in while they were in Tenochtitlán.

Cortés was surprised at the size and beauty of the city. After being in Tenochtitlán for only a few days, Cortés had a plan. He had some of his officers arrest Montezuma. They kept him prisoner in the palace where Cortés was staying. For the next several months, Cortés

Hernán Cortés was surprised by the beauty of Tenochtitlán.

**Cortés and his men met Montezuma and the Aztecs.**

took over ruling Tenochtitlán. He and his men gathered all the gold and silver they could find.

In the spring of 1520, some Aztecs brought news to Cortés. A Spanish fleet had arrived in Mexico, and over 1,000 Spaniards were marching toward Tenochtitlán. Cortés was sure an army from Cuba was coming to arrest him. He took 200 of his men and marched to meet

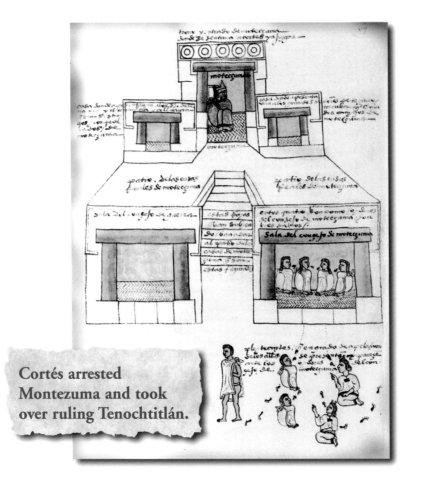

Cortés arrested
Montezuma and took
over ruling Tenochtitlán.

the governor's army. Cortés left a man named Pedro de
Alvarado in charge of the rest of the men. Alvarado was
also in charge of Montezuma and the city of Tenochtitlán.

Cortés knew he could never win a battle against such
a large army, but he had a plan. One night his men
captured the Spaniards who were guarding the camps

of the Cuban governor's army. Cortés told the guards about the large amount of gold that he had gathered in Tenochtitlán. Then he let the guards go back to their camp. The guards hurried to tell the rest of the soldiers about the gold. While this was happening, Cortés and his men captured the leader of the army. Then Cortés talked the rest of the soldiers into joining him. He told them

The Cuban governor's army sailed to Mexico to arrest Cortés. But Cortés had a plan.

## Aztecs and War

Skulls from people that were captured and sacrificed were put on display. Shown here is an Aztec tzompantli, or skull rack.

Fighting in wars was part of religious duty for the Aztec people. They fought to get more land for their empire. They also captured people to sacrifice to their gods. Young Aztec men wanted to be successful warriors. Men who captured many people were given land and other rewards. During battle, the Aztecs used clubs, bows and arrows, and spears. They even had a special spear-throwing device that increased the distance the spears went. The Aztecs wore cotton-padded armor to protect themselves.

they would share in the gold he had stored away in Tenochtitlán.

Cortés, his men, and almost all the men from the governor's army began the long march back to Tenochtitlán.

While Cortés was away, the people of Tenochtitlán held a ceremony for their god of war. Men played drums and people danced and sang. The soldiers feared that the Aztecs were getting ready to attack the palace and free Montezuma. The Spaniards were greatly outnumbered. So, Alvarado had his soldiers fire on the crowd. The Aztecs fought back. They circled the palace where the Spaniards lived and did not let them come out—even to get food and water.

The Aztecs started a ceremony to worship their god of war.

When Cortés returned to Tenochtitlán, the Aztec people were waiting for him.

During the battle between Cortés and the Aztecs, Montezuma was hit in the head.

# A New Mexico

The Aztecs watched as Cortés returned to his palace in Tenochtitlán. Then, thousands began to attack the palace. Cortés brought Montezuma to the roof of the palace. Montezuma talked to the Aztecs below and tried to get them to stop the attack. The Aztecs began throwing stones and Montezuma was hit in the head. He was badly hurt and died three days later.

The Aztecs continued to surround the palace. Cortés knew that his men would soon run out of food and water. He planned an escape. During a stormy night, he told his men to take all the gold they wanted. Then they quietly began leaving the city. The Aztecs discovered the escape. A great battle began. It lasted all night. Over one thousand Spaniards, and maybe as many Aztecs, were killed. The gold that the Spaniards took sank to the bottom of the lake around Tenochtitlán. Cortés and about 400 soldiers escaped. It was the night of June 30, 1520. That night is remembered as noche triste, "the night of tears" or "the sad night."

Cortés and his men hurried to a friendly town miles away from Tenochtitlán. Here they were given food and shelter. Cortés wanted to go back to Tenochtitlán.

Montezuma died three days after the battle.

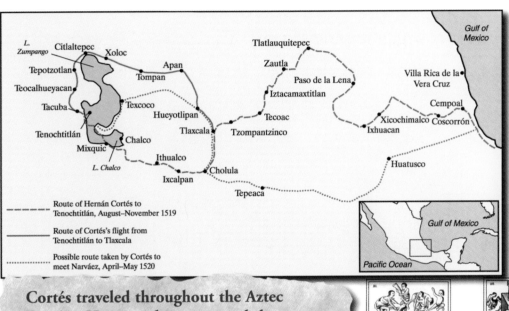

Route of Hernán Cortés to
Tenochtitlán, August–November 1519

Route of Cortés's flight from
Tenochtitlán to Tlaxcala

Possible route taken by Cortés to
meet Narváez, April–May 1520

Cortés traveled throughout the Aztec
Empire. Here are the routes and the names
of the towns through which he passed.

He sent for more men and supplies from Hispaniola.

The Spaniards unknowingly brought smallpox to the Aztecs. After Cortés escaped from Tenochtitlán, people began dying from smallpox. Thousands died and thousands more were left too weak to work or fight.

In May 1521, Cortés and his army returned to Tenochtitlán. They

The Spaniards brought smallpox to the Aztec. The Aztec people did not know about smallpox and many soon died from it.

Cortés and his men returned to Tenochtitlán and surrounded the city. The Aztecs finally gave up. Cortés went on to capture the rest of Mexico.

destroyed the water system so that no fresh water could reach the city. Then they surrounded the city for almost three months. No food or water was brought into the city. The Aztec people, weakened by smallpox and no food, finally gave up.

Cortés and his army captured the rest of the known area of Mexico. Cortés sent many shiploads of gold to the king of Spain. But he kept a large amount of gold for himself. He also owned a lot of land in Mexico.

He was very rich. Cortés was welcomed as a hero when he returned to Spain in 1528.

Later, Cortés sent two expeditions to Mexico to search for gold. But they did not find any. In 1530, Cortés returned to Mexico to search for gold. This expedition also failed to find gold.

By now, Cortés had spent all his money. He returned to Spain in 1540 and found that he had lost favor with the king. Cortés died a poor man

Cortés had a big impact on the people of Mexico. Christianity spread and many churches and cathedrals were built.

Spanish cathedrals were built on Aztec ruins.

on December 2, 1547 near Seville, Spain.

Cortés was cruel to the people of Mexico. He was a fearless explorer and a great general. In 1566, Cortés's body was brought from Spain to be buried in Mexico City.

Cortés brought Christianity to the Aztec people. Cortés and his men destroyed Tenochtitlán and its temples. They built Mexico City on the ruins. Many centuries later, experts in archaeology uncovered the Great Temple in downtown Mexico City. They also found many items, such as art, pottery, and jewelry. Many of these items can now be seen in museums.

This Aztec altar was found during the building of Mexico City's subway system.

# Timeline

**1485**—Hernán Cortés is born in Medellín, Spain.

**1499**—Studies law at the university in Salamanca, Spain.

**1504**—Sails to Hispaniola.

**1511**—Helps conquer the island of Cuba, and claims the land for Spain.

**1519**—Marches to the Aztec city of Tenochtitlán.

**1520**—Montezuma is killed, and Cortés escapes from Tenochtitlán.

**1521**—Conquers the Aztecs.

**May 1528**—Returns to Spain and is hailed as a hero.

**December 2, 1547**—Hernán Cortés dies near Seville, Spain.

**1566**—The body of Cortés is brought from Spain to be buried in Mexico City.

# Words to Know

**archaeology**—The study of the way humans lived a long time ago.

**Christianity**—A religion based on the teachings of Jesus Christ.

**colony**—A group of people who leave their own country and settle in another land.

**conquer**—To overcome or defeat.

**council**—A group of people who gather to give advice or to make rules.

**disease**—A sickness or an illness.

**expedition**—A journey or voyage taken for a special purpose such as to find something or to learn something.

**smallpox**—A disease caused by a virus.

# Learn More About
# Hernán Cortés

## Books

Baquedano, Elizabeth. *Aztec and Inca*. Bethany, Mo.: Fitzgerald Books, 2001.

Donaldson-Forbes, Jeff. *Hernan Cortes*. New York, N.Y.: Rosen Publishing Group, Inc., 2002.

Kimmel, Eric. *Montezuma and the Fall of the Aztecs*. New York, N.Y.: Holiday House, 2000.

Southwater Staff. *Find Out About the Aztecs and Maya: What Life Was Like for Ancient Civilizations in Central America*. London, England: Anness Publishing, 2001.

# Learn More About
# Hernán Cortés

## Internet Addresses

### The City of Tenochtitlán; The Temple and Palaces of the Aztecs

<http://www.rose-hulman.edu/~delacova/aztecs/aztecs21.gif>

<http://www.rose-hulman.edu/~delacova/aztecs/aztecs44.gif>

*At these Web sites, you can find what Tenochtitlán might have looked like.*

### Conquistadors: The Fall of the Aztecs

<http://www.pbs.org/conquistadors/cortes/cortes_flat.html>

*Learn more about Hernán Cortés and the Aztecs.*

# Index